The Cup Makers Guild

The Cup Makers Guild

Matthew Dale Jones

For October and London,
My two favorite large child humans

A Seat in the Back

Sam died. It was just his time.

Before his soul departs for that place souls go to when their earthly shells no longer need them, he attends his funeral. As is custom with the recently departed, he arrives early and takes a seat in the back.

Sam watches as people arrive and spread themselves out among the available seats. This helps to make the space seem fuller than it is. Sam recognizes family members, most of them at least, along with some neighbors, old co-workers, and a few classmates from high school. There are even two ex-lovers. The turnout pleases Sam, but he isn't sure why. Mostly he is happy that some people took the time to pay their respects.

After the eulogy and the usual rituals, those in attendance are invited to share a few words about Sam. There is an uncomfortable pause as those gathered roll their eyes towards the ceiling, scanning their memory banks for stories of Sam worth sharing. A perky neighbor stands up and bounds towards the podium. Those sitting nearby can tell the pause was unbearable for her. She is always the first to share in these types of situations.

"Sam was a good neighbor," she says. "He would always feed my cat when I travelled."

She returns to her seat.

Although it was brief, it appears to have done the job of breaking the ice. A co-worker from the bank that Sam worked at for a short spell (before he was let go for taking too many sick days) stands up and makes his way to the podium.

"I admired how Sam never felt the need to show off with his wardrobe. He always looked comfortable."

Next up is an old high school classmate.

"Sam and I had algebra together."

The classmate freezes and appears to be searching for more to say before awkwardly returning to his seat.

Next up is Sam's college girlfriend. Sam leans forward a bit in anticipation.

"Sam was so considerate. I remember he always chewed spearmint gum, which I thought was nice."

Sam was expecting more but is grateful she spoke at all. He searches his pockets for some gum but finds none.

"Sam always had the newest and best television, and he always sprung for the top-tier cable package. I loved watching movies at his place."

This is Sam's cousin. He was also Sam's cable technician.

After Sam's cousin takes a seat, it is clear nobody else is going to share. The ceremony is considered over, and those that have gathered rise and quietly exit.

Sam watches them as they leave, their faces hiding any emotions that Sam is looking for.

He is now alone, and it is time for him to leave as well. After a couple more required tasks, Sam's soul is headed for that place that souls go to. His time on Earth has come to an end.

Not long after, Sally died too. Like Sam, she takes a seat in the back.

Sally recognizes the attendees from all the different sectors and eras of her time on Earth. She is pleased to see people reconnecting that haven't seen each other in a while, old classmates and co-workers sitting together and catching up before the ceremony kicks off.

Her family, including her children and grandchildren, are sitting up front. They are all wearing blue, her favorite color. This makes Sally smile.

With the eulogy and rituals concluded, it is time to share stories about Sally.

A small woman that walks with a cane stands bolt upright and marches to the podium.

"I'll never forget when Sally came and sat next to me in the cafeteria. I was new to the area and terribly alone and shy. She made me feel welcome, and she didn't care that some kids were snickering at her."

A tall, graceful woman is next.

"Sally and I played volleyball together for several years. She was the best teammate I ever had. She worked so hard, and it pushed us to give it our all. She was so dang positive all the time, too."

"I'll never forget when my mom was sick," a co-worker explains, "and Sally took it upon herself to organize meals for my family. She also made sure that my work responsibilities were covered while I was gone, allowing me to focus on my mom."

"I don't think people realize just how funny Sally was. She would tell stories that would have us all in stitches," a college roommate shares. "I really should have asked her to reimburse me for all of the extra cleaning she caused me from how often I peed my pants because of her stories." This leads to a round of laughter and a few people needing to start some laundry sooner than they planned to.

A very distinguished, white-haired gentleman in a smart-looking suit and tie is next.

"Sally was an incredible problem solver. She was able to look at things from angles none of us could perceive, and it led to her discovering solutions that were unique and highly effective. I learned a lot from Sally."

The sharing portion of the ceremony continues for some time, everyone assembled having multiple stories they want to share, each story prompting head nods as people connect with what is being said.

When it is finally time for Sally's funeral to end, everyone rises, their hearts full, their faces tired from all the crying and laughing, and they exit.

It is now time for Sally to complete her final tasks before her soul departs for that place that souls go to.

Sitting next to her on the back bench is a large, trophy-style cup. It is made from some kind of brushed metal, with two ornate handles and an artfully carved pedestal. "Sally" is etched into the base. It is well used, with dings and worn sections, and it is heavy and sturdy. Sally, however, can lift it easily. It is as if it is a part of her, a part she no longer needs.

She exits the main hall and enters the foyer. In the center sits a large, circular wooden table that appears empty to the Earth-bound. Sally places her cup on the table, hoisting it from her hip. It lands with a deep thud only she can hear. She notices another cup on the table, a modest goblet with a smooth, plain surface. "Sam" is scratched into its side. Next to it is a small book that doesn't appear to have been cracked open, crisp as the day it was pressed.

Seeing the book reminds Sally to reach into her back pocket and extract her copy of that same book. Hers has seen better days. It is creased and weathered; several of the pages no longer attached to the spine. It is heavily marked up too, with notes on every page. The notes aren't all from the same utensil, Sally having revisited the text over the years, adding new notes as new thoughts and understandings came to her.

Like the cup, she no longer needs the book. She plops it down on the table.

Her final tasks complete, Sally pushes open the heavy door and enters that place souls go to.

The Cup Makers Guild

Prologue

The world is full of speeches
That are given at the end,
But with these words I hope to put a dent
Into that trend.
The way I see it, at the end,
Well, that's kind of late!
Not everybody makes it there,
And that's unfortu-nate.

The start is where these words belong,

With everybody there,

So, everyone can hear the news

And use it to prepare.

What I'm about to share

May challenge you to comprehend,

But if you do,

And use it too,

Then you just might transcend.

Chapter 1

The Oath

Stop!

Don't go any further!

I need a validation,

That you've progressed in life at least to

8th grade graduation.

I'll use the honor system,

But I'd prefer a urine sample,

Or a lock of hair for DNA

I would also see as ample

Proof that you are old enough to hear

The secrets found within,

That once you learn may hurt your head,

If so, take aspirin.

We've wasted enough time already,

So, raise your right hand please,

And repeat this phrase that I think may come

Straight from Socrates:

I swear I will examine,

My life from head to toe,

I'll read this book from front to back,

I have a right to know,

The secrets that await me

As I move forward on my trip,

Through four sacred years of high school

That will go by like a blip.

The knowledge that awaits me
Will have an impact,
That's for sure,
On whether I excel at life
And spend it quite secure,
Or whether I will struggle,
More than what seems fair,
So, I swear to read this closely,
On my honor,
I declare.

Chapter 2

The Truth About High School

Congratulations!

You made it!

A graduate of 8th grade!

You are the Grand Marshal

Of the Finisher's Parade!

You are now prepared

To hear about what lies ahead,

The truth about high school,

That oh so many dread.

You may believe that it will feel

Like four years of detention,

Or just more of what has come before,

A junior high extension.

But here's the truth—it's none of those things!

It's where grown-up life gets a foreshadowing!

The work you do in high school is important,

Yes, it's true,

But not for the reasons

That you always thought you knew.

Like taking English to learn Shakespeare,

Or Math to fix up numbers,

Or History to make sure

That you don't repeat those blunders.

You're going to be freer,
You'll have more room to roam,
And more and more time
Will be spent away from home.
You will develop your own style,
Spend more time with your friends,
You'll start yearning for the time
When these freedoms can extend.

To driving a car!

Or staying out late!

You're itching for that day

When you emancipate!

To strike out on your own,

100% free!

To be seen as an adult,

Undoubtedly!

But it's more than just aging or learning to drive,
This act of maturing and living to thrive.
It's about being responsible,
Knowing what's true,
It's about doing good work,
Not just getting tattoos!

This is why there's high school,

For four years in your teens,

To run you through some challenges,

And study your routines.

You're going to do a lot of work,

And many choices you will make,

And will you be dependable,

Or will you be a flake?

Herein lies the truth

That you're now old enough to hear,

But it cannot leave this book,

I need to make that clear.

You're in a special group,

So, you have a right to know,

About the CUPS,

About the GUILD,

And what you'll undergo.

Chapter 3

The Cups

Each adult that has ever lived
Carried a cup with them.
The Romans did,
Egyptians too,
Even those in Bethlehem.
All around the world,
In every country and every town,
Each adult has a cup with them,
And they never put it down.

It's natural to be confused,

It's reasonable to have doubts,

And I know you're probably thinking,

"What the BLEEP are you talking about?!"

To really understand the cups,

To grasp what all this means,

You first have to believe me,

Well, the cups?

They are unseen.

While nobody can see their cup,

They know that it's there,

Kind of like a tighty-whitey pair of underwear,

That help to keep some things in place,

And keep your pants clean,

Especially on days

When you've had way too much caffeine!

The cups have always held exactly what
Someone can do,
Like when they helped great Marco Polo's
Quest for Xanadu.
See cups have led to greatness,
As well as the demise,
Of people that ignored their cups
And the limits of its size.

Everything goes in the cup,

You use it every day,

Making your bed,

Brushing your teeth,

Mowing the lawn *before* you play.

The cup is good for holding things,

Like holding in a fart,

That if you didn't hold it,

Other things would fall apart.

Relationships may tatter,

Your reputation ripped to shreds,

A messy house,

Low bank account,

A garden that's all dead,

Are outcomes that are possible

When we fail to do our job,

Of using our cups wisely

And instead become a slob.

It all comes down to cup size,

I want to make that clear,

For you to make the most of life,

For you to persevere.

To enjoy the highs and handle the lows,

And live to tell the tale,

You cannot have a small cup

That will leave you feeling frail.

I hate to say it,

And the thought gives me the chills,

But life with a small cup

Will lead to so many more spills.

Like failing to show up on time

Because you fell asleep,

Or saying inappropriate things

And being labeled "that weird creep."

I believe I need to clarify,

Perhaps I overstated,

When I said "everything,"

Well, I might have exaggerated.

Everything IMPORTANT

Is what I should have said,

Like saving hard earned money

For a rainy day ahead.

Everything *important* goes in,

But only if it fits,

Like learning how to drive a car

By earning your permit,

Or taking a vacation,

Or buying your first house,

Or learning how to share it

With your one and only spouse.

Easy things,

Like laying down,

Or watching the TV,

Don't require any effort,

Hardly burn a calorie.

These actions that don't grow us,

Don't take us anywhere,

Don't need to fit into your cup,

That's a fact I need to share.

A life spent doing easy things,

Cup-LESS activities,

Will feel like you're stuck in a zoo,

You're in captivity.

You might think…Cool!

I get free food!

And a place to sleep!

But those four walls are really tall,

Impossible to leap.

An active life spent doing,

And one that you control,

Is one that's filled with purpose,

One that feeds the soul.

That's why our cups are vital,

They build our self-esteem,

And they support a life

Where we get to pursue our dreams!

We go as far as we can go,

Fly high as we can fly!

But the limits of our cup

We have no choice but to comply.

So, let's review about the cups

That you are soon to get,

That you earn by what you SAY and DO,

Not luck like in roulette.

They help us do important things,

They support us on our way,

And small cups often lead to lives

Awash in disarray.

Now you're probably wondering,

"Where do the cups come from?"

You are in luck!

Because that is next up,

In this curriculum.

They are made by a secret group,

That watches all you do,

And just like tales of Santa Claus,

It's hard to tell what's true.

Chapter 4

The Cup Makers Guild

The Cup Makers Guild
Will make cups for you all,
As they work in near silence
Up in Cup Makers' Hall.
They chisel and shape,
And they polish and mold,
And their work is impeccable,
Or so I've been told.

What we know of the Makers

Can qualify as theory,

The mysteries surrounding them

Have led many to query.

Who are they?

Where'd they come from?

The questions never ending.

The truth is we may never know,

Our disbelief just needs suspending.

We know that they're an ancient group,

Origin unknown,

Their handiwork and history

Are together neatly sewn.

Since sapiens have walked this earth,

They've been making cups,

That find their way to human hands

When they become grown up.

They never show their faces,

They're a stealthy,

Shrouded clan,

With well-constructed Halls

In London,

New York,

and Japan.

With outlets set up everywhere,

All the whole worldwide,

They witness everything you do,

There's just no way to hide!

It's believed their Halls are spotless,

Organized with many tools,

And notebooks everywhere

For every student in high school.

The notebooks hold the information

That the Makers need,

To make each cup specific

Based upon each student's deeds.

The Cup Makers' work is twofold,

Step one before step two,

Thorough plans must be devised,

For the cup is just for you.

They watch your every action,

Every decision that you make,

Everything that you avoid,

And everything that you partake.

The Makers need to get it right,

The cups they are exact.

They hold only what you can handle,

That's a well-known fact.

When people try to do too much,

They fill and fill and fill,

The cup begins to overflow,

And life begins to spill.

So, whether you are ready,

Or wildly unskilled,

You will leave high school with a cup,

Courtesy of the Guild.

A big cup to handle it,

To love it,

And to thrive?

Or a small cup that leaves you asking,

"How can I survive?"

The challenge set before you
Is to hear the Makers' call,
To work hard,
To be kind,
And don't ever drop the ball.

Chapter 5

The Cup Makers' Call
or How To Earn a Big Cup

High school is where we prove ourselves

To the Cup Makers on the hill,

As they watch how we handle life,

And exercise free will.

Do we give it our best effort?

Do we retreat to beds and screens?

Do we communicate with intelligence?

Or use language that's obscene?

High school can be a hostile place,

Just like the wild frontier,

So, it's important to prepare yourself,

Just like a pioneer.

Be prepared,

Anticipate,

Leave nothing up to chance,

But most of all,

Your character,

Protect with vigilance.

See character and cup size
Share a strong relationship,
It's everything we think and do,
It's like a microchip,
That's programmed with our habits,
Those things we always do,
Like saying "please" when asking,
And when you get,
"Thank you."

It's Aristotle that reminded us,

We are those things we do,

Again and again without thinking much,

We act as if on cue.

We're driven by our habits,

And they develop over time,

And if they're crafted with intention

It can mean a life sublime.

If you can turn GOOD into habit,

Make those choices automatic,

The positive will multiply,

'cuz you made it systematic.

Each system is designed

To get the results that it gets,

Good ones can lead to riches,

While bad ones lead to debts.

See high school is a wondrous place

To grow capacity,

It's also where we shed that skin of immaturity,

But only you can do these things

If you are to grow up,

And graduate with confidence,

Holding a big cup.

If you're given a small cup

And you start to make your way,

And regret how little that it holds,

You'll wish you could replay,

All those times you should have moved,

But instead chose to be still,

And now you're looking at a life

That is exclusively uphill.

While classmates that made different choices,

Tough ones to be sure,

Like doing homework on weekends,

A free time forfeiture,

Are making strides,

Enjoying life,

Their seeds starting to bloom,

While your parents are still wondering why

You're in your childhood room.

The Guild will do exchanges
If you desire a larger cup,
But you'll need to work real hard,
You'll need to play catch up.
You'll need to rectify your errors
You made while in high school,
Those habits that have held you back
You'll need to overrule.

You'll wish you did it earlier,

You'll wish you gave your all,

You'll wish you tried to impress those

That work up in the Hall.

You'll wish for a do over,

You'll wish you made a vow,

To make investments in your character,

Much sooner,

Like right now!

The hard truth is you get the cup
That you have rightly earned.
It's based on everything you did
And what the Makers learned,
Like how you dealt with deadlines,
Or people that rubbed you wrong.
Did you meet them with consistency?
Find a way to get along?

Adults will maybe threaten,

Or smother you with adulation,

But here's the thing you need to know

When it comes to motivation.

That energy to do a thing

Even though you'd rather not,

Is strongest when it comes from you,

In fact, it's fiery hot!

A trick to get you moving,
If you'd like to call it that,
When you're feeling rather cold
And need to pump the thermostat,
Is to imagine YOU in the future,
And what that YOU would think,
If instead of doing the hard work,
You ignore it and you shrink.

If you think the future YOU won't care,

Well, that's rather dumb.

You see, people that think this way

Become quite troublesome.

They only think of themselves,

They only think of now,

And when they fall behind

They make excuses as to how.

Take notice of the adults

That seem to have big cups,

That handle problems calmly,

That rarely, if ever, blow up.

Watch closely how they deal with life,

Soak it like a sponge,

Then emulate their every move…go ahead!

Take the plunge!

Your life is your creation,

The sum total of your choices,

The ones that learn this earliest

Have reason to rejoices.

Each day they wake up gladly,

Salute the rising sun,

And choose to make good choices,

'Cuz a good life is hard won.

Chapter 6

The Ancient Document

You are about to read
The only missive ever sent,
From the Guild down to us humans,
It's an ancient document.
It's intention is to guide us
As we stumble on our way,
From adolescence to adulthood,
They had wisdom to relay.

The Makers are another race,

So, they were quite confused,

About so many of the choices

That we humans seem to choose.

They thought they'd mostly make cups

That were much larger in size,

But the actions of so many

Have forced them to minimize.

So, while the charter clearly stated,
"No communication,"
They got clearance to pass on
This one direct articulation.
It was all that they had learned
From their relentless observation,
It was intended as a guide,
A sort of "good choice" stimulation.

While this document is very old,

It often gets an update,

The text needs to reflect the times,

Some phrases need a translate,

Examples get a refresh,

And language gets cleaned up,

But the message always stays the same—

It's all about your cup.

I can say with confidence

That exposure to this text,

Will open up your eyes

And leave you slightly less perplexed,

About how life works,

And all that you can do,

To make the most of it,

And make the most of you.

Chapter 7

A Message for the
Large Child Humans

For about a decade,

You've been learning,

You've been growing,

With pagey books that needed reading,

And grassy lawns that needed mowing.

There's nothing you don't know

About the ins and outs of school,

So, forgive us when we don't believe

When you act like a fool.

You learned to walk through all the falling,

And all of the crying,

But have you ever seen

A baby human never trying?

Just lying there forever,

Never trying to stand up?

Never facing all life's challenges,

Never earning their prized cup?

High school should be no different
Than your earliest of days,
When you woke up everyday
Intent to set the world ablaze!
First you walked,
And then you talked,
You grew and grew and grew,
The world was your oyster!
There was no stopping you!

Most of your life is spent

Beyond the childhood years,

You know,

Three to one,

Adult to child,

The average ratio.

So, it makes sense to be

The best adult that you can be,

By developing your confidence

And sense of agency.

Believing that you're in control,

That life is in your hands,

Is a powerful belief

That many fail to understand.

It's more likely that they adopt

That convenient attitude,

That "it's just luck,"

Or "who you know,"

Not their ineptitude.

We all control how hard we work,

That thing called elbow grease,

That thing that always has a knack

To properly increase,

The "luck" of finding ourselves

In a pretty good position.

There's nothing that can hold you back

When hard work is your mission!

Success does not fall from the clouds

That fly over Madrid,

It bubbles up from all the work

That starts when you're a kid.

It's dedication,

It's sacrifice,

It's courage in the storm,

To stick to your convictions

Amid attempts to misinform.

Like you only have to do the work

That you happen to like.

And if you don't?

Well that's ok,

Go ride your motorbike!

Or it's ok to post online

Any thought found in your head,

or that rumor of a rumor

That you think is fun to spread.

Now we know you're probably thinking...Hey!

I know adults that bare,

A resemblance to the immature acts

That we just shared.

While it's true that there are adults

That are childish in their ways,

It's not advisable for you

To be their protege.

The childish acts of children
Are expected 'cuz their kids,
But when adults act like children,
There is pain for what they did.
Jobs can be lost,
And spouses too,
It can really bruise the soul,
When adults fail to use
That crucial trait of self-control.

The truth is that it's hard to use

Something you never gain,

That's why when you're in high school

It is vital that you train,

By corralling those wild impulses

That evidence will show,

Will determine the direction

That your life will tend to go.

So, pay attention!

Open your eyes!

To how often you respond,

In a way that is in service

To the days that lie beyond.

But if you find that you

Can only focus on right now,

You may find that you'll receive

The smallest cup that we allow.

Now don't think the expectation
Is all work and never play,
But growing up is as much
About tomorrow as today.
Today is called the present
And tomorrow is a gift,
But only if you plan for it,
And don't spend today adrift.

Balancing the here and now,

Along with days to come,

Is a mature act that aims

To live a life at maximum.

Enjoy the moment!

Plan for the future!

You need to do them both,

If you're to experience a life

That has continued growth.

It's true that we all have those things

That we would rather do,

Like eating a crumb donut,

Or shopping for more shoes.

Or staying in our cozy bed

As long as we'd like,

Or drawing,

Or dancing,

Or riding our red bike.

But something that we at the Guild

Really like to see,

Is when you start to exercise

Advanced maturity.

Like when you learn to balance

All the work and all the fun,

By spending time on your phone

After all the homework's done.

But when you flat out refuse,

Or ignore the work that's there,

Throw off a lazy vibe

And maybe snort,

"I just don't care!"

Or "I'm bored" is a flippant phrase

That's too often heard,

Falling from the lips

Of the annoyingly absurd.

For boredom we invented,

It is of our favorite test,

Along with having you show up

A wee bit underdressed,

Or having your crush laugh out loud

At your sincere request,

And it all leaves you feeling

At your utmost loneliest.

If you believe that Steve Jobs

Masterminded the smart phone,

We need to break it to you,

That's an invention that we own.

Football is us,

Video games too,

And makeup makes us proud,

Along with all the silly apps

You download from the cloud.

See, these are challenges

That we on purpose throw your way,

To coincide with Mrs. Jones

Assigning that essay.

The challenge makes you stronger,

Forces you to choose,

That's why it's so important

To fight through and not refuse.

The obstacle becomes the way,

You make adjustments and proceed,

Acceptance of the challenge

Makes you unstoppable,

Yes indeed!

Knowing there's a purpose,

Something bigger going on,

Can give you all the strength you need

To win this marathon!

While this news may arouse in you

Severe dissatisfaction,

Like in third grade when you were told

You had to learn your fractions,

We hope you're not discouraged,

Or feeling rather glum —

Take a deep breath,

And embrace,

The challenges to come.

Take it all in stride,

And don't ever feel defeated,

Never act conceited,

Or feel that you've been cheated.

Instead force a smile

To curl the corners of your lips,

And remember all of the Cup Makers'

Cup-growing tips —

That high school is a game

Crafted especially for you,

To help you grow the skills you need

To actively pursue,

The best life you can ever have,

One that fills you up,

The life you love because you earned it

With your big, fat cup!

So, if you're ever late

Because your car got a flat tire,

Or nervousness about that speech

Causes droplets of perspire,

Remember that that moment

Was intended to inspire,

To challenge you to overcome,

To light your inside fire!

That fire that will fuel your journey,

From child to adult,

A journey through the years

That can be deeply difficult.

Always know it's not intended

To leave you feeling bad,

Or sulky sad,

Or mangy mad,

Or at odds with your dad.

These tough years will prep you
For adulting all alone,
To cast off those training wheels,
And join the fully grown!
To have a job,
Pay all your bills,
And buy a zoomy car!
To be Employee of the Year
And win a trip to Zanzibar!

But they'll also get you ready

For the lower moments too,

Like going to the DMV

And enduring their long queue,

Or appointments with the taxman

And the news he likes to share,

That your bank account will shrink

A little more than what seems fair.

Let's end our time together
With a summarized review,
A super, duper list
Of tips and acts that you can do.
Ideas that work for everyone,
From Maine to Idaho,
On how to earn your big, big cup…
Ok, here we go!

Your work comes first,

And play comes later.

Do it first thing,

And don't be a wait-er.

Surround yourself with people you trust,

And steer clear of those that earn your disgust.

Get involved and try new things!

Pay close attention to your teachers' lecturings!

Hold your tongue, and wait your turn,

And do everything in your power to learn

The names of your teachers, and classmates too.

And always say "bless you,"

When you hear an, "a-choo!"

Take care of your body,

Take care of your soul,

Exercise moderation and stay in control.

So just do it already!

Start growing your cup!

And if you're behind,

Well hurry!

Catch up!

These four years go fast,

Trust us it's true,

Embrace every moment,

And do all you can do!

Chapter 8

So, Now You Know

So,

Now you know the secret,

About the Cups,

About the Guild,

About the tests of high school

And the character they build.

But knowledge of a thing

Is only where a tale begins,

Turning knowledge into actions

Will demand your discipline.

You are the only person

That will be there every day,

To keep things moving forward,

Or to let them slip away.

Engage in your own progress!

Don't wait to be told!

Be the artist of your life,

For it is yours to mold.

Life is a beautiful challenge

You see,

One that requires your tenacity,

Your tireless effort,

Your positive attitude,

A reasonable relationship

With fatty fast food.

Perfection is not the Cup Makers' concern,

They just want to see

That you're starting to learn,

That your life is your own,

You are the caretaker,

Your dreams can come true

Because you are their maker!

So, I bid you farewell,

And good luck on your trip,

I have faith you'll do well,

'Cuz you have a good grip,

On the task set before you,

And all that it means,

To grow a good life,

And how that starts in your teens.

Epilogue

To be honest,

As they like to say,

I told a small white lie.

The Cup Makers Guild is a fabrication,

But let me clarify.

There are no halls,

There are no notes,

There are no cups, it's true.

The Cup Maker that will make your "cup,"

Well, in fact,

It's you!

I wrote this allegory

As a way to help you sail,

Through the challenges of high school

By transporting to this tale.

While the stuff about the cups is false,

The metaphor is true,

That we build cup-acity

To get through all the things we do.

High school is like a gym for life,

And like most gyms I know,

If you make the most of your time there,

You'll turn into a pro!

But I know there will be days

When you are not feeling it,

When your fire isn't burning hot

And you couldn't give a...poop.

It's those days when you need a lift,

A bit of fantasy,

To supply you with some fuel to move,

A shot of energy.

Think of the Cup Makers taking notes

Up there in their Hall,

And whether your cup will be big,

Or whether it be small.

Sometimes our motivation

Can be found in funny places,

Like imagining we're being chased

To go faster in our races.

But that's ok,

In fact it works,

Our brains are pretty strong,

At finding clever ways

To help us as we get along.

Forgive me if I took too long

To make a simple point,

At the very least I hope this story

Did not disappoint.

Now it's time to close this book,

And I wish you well,

It's time for you to write your story…

Which one will you tell?

Matthew Dales Jones lives with his wife Laurie in California. They teach at the same high school and were co-hosts of the Teacher Saves World! podcast. They have two children. Matthew is the author of one other book, *Helping Teens Succeed in High School & Life for Parents & Teachers*.

He can be reached at:
teachersavesworld@gmail.com

Made in the USA
Las Vegas, NV
28 January 2024

84983929R00080